NOISE FROM THE UNDER- GROUND

a secret history
of alternative
ROCK

NOISE

FROM THE

UNDER-
GROUND

Photographs by Michael Lavine

Text by Pat Blashill

With an Introduction by Henry Rollins

Simon & Schuster Editions
A Fireside Book

PUBLISHED BY SIMON & SCHUSTER, INC.

FIRESIDE
Rockefeller Center
1230 Avenue of the Americas
New York, New York 10020

FIRESIDE and colophon are registered trademarks
of **Simon & Schuster Inc.**

Book and Cover design:
David Carson **Assisted by**
Tina Meyers and Christa Skinner

Printed in Hong Kong by South China Printing (1988) LTD
10 9 8 7 6 5 4 3 2 1
Library of Congress Cataloging-In-Publication Data

Blashill, Pat.
    Noise from the Underground: a secret history of alternative rock/photographs by Michael Lavine;
    text by Pat Blashill; with an introduction by Henry Rollins.
    p. cm.
    "Simon & Schuster Editions."
    Discography: p.***
    1. Alternative rock music–History and criticism. 2. Alternative rock musicians–Portraits. I. Lavine,
    Michael. II. Title.
ML3534.B63 1996
781.66–dc20   96–19373
ISBN 0-684-81513-3   CIP
                                    MN

For Laurie & Olive
In memory of Steve Brown

Contents

Acknowledgments

"DIDN'T I SEE YOU AT THE BLACK FLAG SHOW LAST NIGHT?" I SAID TO THE GIRL WITH THE CURLY RED HAIR AS WE STOOD IN LINE AT THE SCHOOL CAFETERIA IN NEW YORK. Since both of us were **members of a secret club** called the "INDIE ROCK SCENE," we instantly bonded, and after talking for a bit, the girl asked me if I would photograph her band, White Zombie. *Psycho Head Blowout* was my first album cover and my point of entry into the world of rock-and-roll photography; it was also the **beginning of a successful merger between** my love for photography and my love for rock and *roll.*

A few years later, my friend Bruce Pavitt called to say he had just signed a new band named Nirvana. "And they're going to be HUGE!" he said. "Come on, Bruce," I said, "you say that about all your bands." Not really believing his own hype anymore, we both agreed that there was just no way any of his bands would ever be as big as, say, Guns n' Roses. Boy, were we wrong!

WE DIDN'T KNOW THAT OUR SECRET CLUB WOULD EVER BE DUG UP. We had no idea that this music would be discovered by the rest of the world. But when the explosion happened, I found myself right in the middle of it all, and I consider myself lucky to be involved in such an exciting time in rock and roll.

 *I would like to thank* the people who helped put this book together. To my agent, Stephen Pevner; my editor, Anne Yarowsky; Schneider/Erdman and Anthony Accardia at Green Rhino for their incredible printing; and to Lisa Ross for helping me organize the massive amount of photographic material.

Many thanks are also due to Bruce Pavitt for his continued support; F-stop Fitzgerald, Katy Swann, Mary Rozzi, Ken Berland, Wendy Schwartz, Michelle Kelling, Madelana Polletta, the crew at Outline/Edge, Steven Johnson, Simon Reynolds, Francesco Scavullo, Mark Arm, Kurt and Courtney, Terry Tolkin, Keith Wood, Janet Billig, Paul Smith, Sonic Youth, Jon Spencer, Christina Martinez, Steve Bush, Dave Todd, Brad Sweek, Richard Kern, and of course all of the bands. I would also like to thank my family back in Colorado and California, and my wife, Laurie, and my daughter, Olive.

—M. L.

And up next we have an introduction to
an alternative rock book by a man hurtling toward forty with graying hair and fading tattoos, who still goes onstage with a band, *jumps*  UP and down, and screams.

by Henry Rollins

As far as I can tell. The alternative/punk-rock music world has always struggled for credibility and respect. Often this struggle outshadowed the need to write good songs. You spent a lot of the time hustlin'. There were times when you just couldn't get your music heard by anyone outside a few select people in cities scattered all over the country. You would get in the van and play the endless connect-the-dots drive game from dive to dive with your Xeroxed, single-sheet tour itinerary lost somewhere on the dashboard along with the few pages of the atlas that still remained. You would haul your music all over the place just to get it heard, to not be invisible, or, worse, rendered silent.

Henry Rollins

New York City,
1991

The struggles were cool and infuriating. Listening to the radio and hearing the bilge that was bombarding millions of could-be fans instead of the music that you had been starving and working on so devotedly to make exist was hard at times. The adversity became part of the music, part of the attitude. For some bands, the struggle styled the music. This was sometimes good, often not. That character-building stuff runs a little thin sometimes.

The records were usually low-fi because there was often not enough budget to allow the bands to realize their vision. Sometimes I would listen to a record knowing that the band was frustrated by this and wondered what the music would have sounded like if they could have had a real production budget. The recording contracts were often criminal. A band would sign on the dotted line (if there was one to sign on; many small-label "contracts" are still locked up in he-said-she-said verbal agreements/arguments that are over a decade old) for a few months' rent, not realizing they had given away half of their publishing rights and who-the-hell-knows-what-else. The naive and soulful energy of these artists was often turned against them, and the result was a breakup and enough bitterness to cause a power outage in a major city.

The press coverage of the music was at times wildly insulting and uninformed. The music was treated like a curiosity piece, and the band members were treated like strange brats who had funny hair-cuts and had not yet settled down to becoming good Americans, but aren't they cute anyway. Sometimes when the band would come to town they were considered a hazard by the local police force, which often threatened violence, arrest, or impoundment of equipment. Shows were often picketed by strange herds of sign-carrying women, high on daytime TV paranoia and Dexatrim, angrily protesting the band's music, which they probably hadn't heard anyway but could blame their families' dysfunction and the whole damn country's moral decay upon. It was a small wake-up call for the ignorant and it put the spotlight on the powers-that-be in all their out-of-touch glory.

oductio

The original alternative bands had to stand up hard for what they believed in. Imagine someone telling you that your work sucks and waving the *Frampton Comes Alive!* album at you and asking why you can't play some REAL music like this. A guy once told me that when the Stooges' *Raw Power* album came out, people would bring it to parties as a joke so they could put it on and crack up laughing. I never thought that record was a laughing matter.

At one point it seemed that it was the music that no one wanted. Record companies were too busy struggling to coax their aging, seventies-era acts into the limo to the enormo-dome to prop up the falling arches of what so gloriously was. The balding men with the ponytails and cowboy boots driving in their BMWs with the AC cranked were not going to give up any ground and just didn't want to know. A guy with big hair was croaking out something unintelligible, and that was all there was happening in the music industry today, thank you. Good studios were out of the question for most alternative bands, as more often than not were good producers, engineers, sound and light companies, venues, you name it. Not to put them down, but Van Halen, Zep, and the Rolling Stones were not told to fuck off and go away for years and years. They. Just. Weren't.

Yet, there at the end of the line, in the midst of the rip-offs and incredibly inept media (which put permanent doubts as to the veracity of ANY adult's say-so), there was always the music. Which only a few years ago actually got heard on a level that it so achingly deserved. And the music has somehow persevered not so politely or patiently, thank god, waiting for time and the record companies to slowly see that they can make a buck, rock some more of those three-hour lunches, and pat themselves on the back for pioneering what X termed "The Unheard Music."

Poster for **Daydream Nation** (Blast First Records), August 1988

So things have changed . . . somewhat. And for now, that is the reality we are living in. Young people are working in major record companies and are being given the chance to get some great music out. Major labels are taking baby steps (I wish MTV would get up off their ass and take some too), and some great bands are getting heard, and even the small labels are getting the records out and not getting stiffed so brutally by late or nonpaying distributors. I am the last person to say that all is well in the music world—there is still the unrelenting tonnage of crap in every genre coming out year after year, and I suspect there always will be. But the way "alternative" music is seen is different these days, and that's where a fine fellow like Michael Lavine comes in. He's one of the good guys. Just by the respect he gives the artists and the sheer quality of his artistry, he's one of the good eggs who gives much-needed legitimacy to a music scene that so totally deserves it.

It wouldn't matter if all he did was do photos for travel guides, the guy ·is a tremendous artist, and his work is immediately recognizable, and in my opinion, it is often copied. The fact that Michael loves and, more importantly, understands this music is entirely evident in the work in this book.

There's something that he captures about the bands and the people that is wonderful and unique. It's as if he is their biggest fan and has the uncanny ability to bring out the unseen from a crew that like to have holes in their jeans and don't always pride themselves on being fashion mavens. Hell, there's some art right there.

And the ideas he comes up with. I mean, come on, how about that Dwarves album cover? All the great stuff he has done with Sonic Youth? The list goes on as you turn the pages. The energy he puts into the work is excellent. It takes much more than a band just showing up for a photo session for the whole thing to really rock. The "thing" has to be there, and that's what separates the great from the common. It might be your music and your band, but when you work with Michael, it's HIS session (although you would never know it), and it's a good place to be, because he gets it, obviously.

—Henry Rollins
1995

Nirvana
album session for **Nevermind** (DGC) May 1991

by Pat Blashill

a fan's NOTES

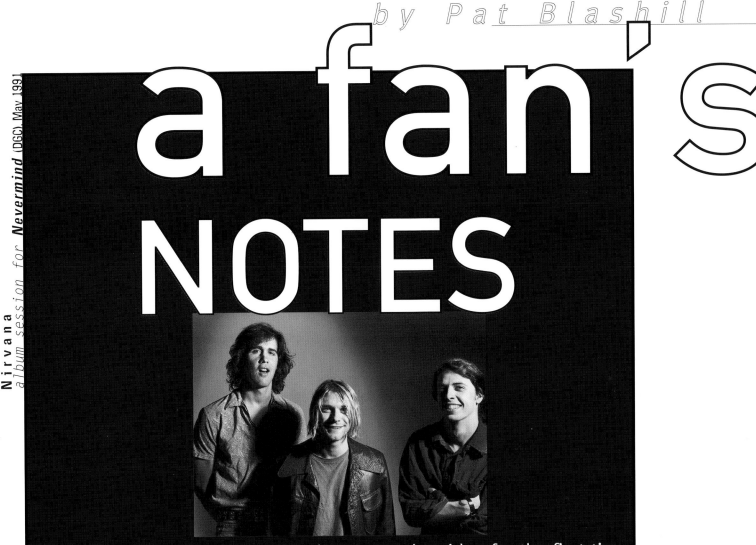

I remember exactly where I was when I saw the video for the first time. I was in a grotty little hotel pub in Scotland, hanging out with a frayed-at-the-cuffs indie-pop band, the shamblingly brilliant Teenage Fanclub.

At one point I bumbled by the bar's wide-screen television, and it was showing the video clip for Nirvana's "Smells Like Teen Spirit," which I'd heard was becoming very popular back in the United States. The video was filled with punk-rock cheerleaders, crowd surfing, and anarchy, and it looked like surveillance camera footage of a vast and ferocious underground, like pictures of a whole subculture that had always existed but had never been spoken of or spoken to. It looked like a riot that had been waiting to happen.

I was an eyewitness to the birth of the Alternative Nation. And the *death of the American punk-rock underground.*

Nirvana

publicity session with **Chad Channing**
(Sub Pop), April 1990

*Use the word **"alternative"** around anyone under twenty-five, and you will see that kid* wince. It's the instinctual shudder of someone rejecting a pat definition of his generation. "Alternative" may be the only word we have to describe a culture that straggled up through the cracks in the pavement of Main Street, but somehow it's not enough. Never before has a word as colorless as "alternative"

Liz Phair

publicity
session
(Matador Records),
January 1994

been bandied about to describe such a crazy panoply of best-selling musical artists, including everyone from an odd, confessional singer/songwriter named Liz Phair to a martini-swilling glam-rock band called Urge Overkill. NEVER BEFORE HAS A WORD BEEN SO INADEQUATE AND *OVERSTRETCHED* AND CARELESSLY APPLIED TO SUCH A BROAD SPEC-TRUM OF CULTURAL PHENOMENA as suburban skateboarding, mall tattoo parlors, the rise of fanzines, and the pop-ularity of homegrown, independent films like *Clerks*. And never before has such an unappetizing word been employed to sell youth culture back to the people who invented it in the first place. Besides, *"alternative" is now a misnomer.*

nirvana

Today alternative describes the tastes and predilections of mainstream American youth.

But alternative culture *wasn't* invented by Nirvana in 1992. They just brought an anthem of disaffection and anger to the top of the charts, to the malls, to the army bases, and into the living rooms of a nation that had spent most of the eighties trying to convince itself that it was a kind and *gentle place.*

In the *EIGHTIES,* America was all about **shiny** surfaces, and mainstream culture was about as deep as Bobby McFerrin's 1988 hit song, "Don't Worry Be Happy." Movies like *Back to the Future* and *Romancing the Stone* weren't the norm, just sure signs that Hollywood was again becoming a factory for empty escapism. The best-seller lists were rocked by *Slaves of New York, Less Than Zero,* and **Bright Lights,** *Big City,* three very hip novels about people with nice clothes, cocaine, and hardly anything to say.

The Fluid

publicity session (Sub Pop), March 1988

Charlotte, North Carolina, April 1992

Pearl Jam

ALTERNATIVE CULTURE IN THIS COUNTRY BEGAN AS AN ATTEMPT TO GET TO THE TRUTH AND BEAU-TY **BENEATH THE POLISHED SURFACES OF AMERICAN MAINSTREAM THOUGHT AND ART.** This wasn't a new impulse—it was the very same mission that has driven bohemian *under-ground movements,* both here and abroad, throughout this century.

So what does it mean today to see Pearl Jam's Eddie Vedder wearing a Minor Threat punk-rock T-shirt? It means that he is acting out one of the most inexorable impulses of indie rock—that is, the fiendish desire to turn anyone who will listen on to something new: a band they might not have heard, a magazine they didn't know about, a snowboard shop they've never seen. It means that Eddie is a fan, not just someone who inspires fans. The rock T-shirt is the sartorial shorthand of our generation. It says, "I like this music—I am this culture." No other explanation from the wearer is necessary.

Unsane

New York City,
1987

Alternative music makes virtues out of the vices that mainstream pop and rock previously tried to avoid. The bands *use guitar* D I S T O R T I O N not just as a musical device, but as a medium unto itself, and they make noise that is as expressive as a PLAYGROUND MELODY. They use murky production and effects as a way of evoking atmosphere. They play with old drum kits and transistor amplifiers because that gives the music a warm, human sound. Because of these things, alternative rock *sounds* like the polar

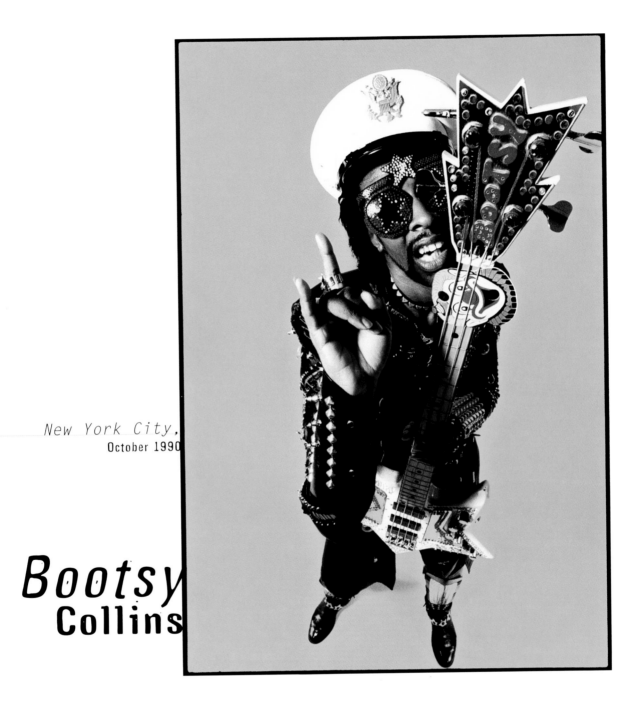

New York City,
October 1990

Bootsy
Collins

opposite of the ultraslick top pop that dominated radio and MTV in the eighties. This music, much of which was released initially on *i n d e p e n d e n t   l a b e l s* and played to small but fervent audiences, is no longer an underground phenomenon. Yet texturally, it still sounds slightly subterranean, like something repressed that crawled up from beneath the boards of the American bandstand. In a sense, this is still underground music because it sounds, feels, and looks dirty.

The same idea applies to everything in alternative or indie culture besides the music. Indie style—the clothes, the poster art for concerts, the movies that Nirvana fans embrace—is all about entropy, about the underside of a **b l a n d** Norman Rockwell dream. That's why Hüsker Dü titled one of their albums *Everything Falls Apart*. That's why White Zombie fans dress like the band—with matted dreadlocks, dirty-ass torn jeans, and motorcycle boots taped together with duct tape. That's why a major studio movie like *Reality Bites*, produced to appeal to and exploit alternative-rock fans, features a key scene in a convenience store, the quintessential marketplace of nineties fast-food garbage culture. And that's why long hair, originally a sign of effeminate defiance, is now almost purely a gesture of evasion, refusal and *disengagement*. Worn by an indie rock kid, long hair is just a shade, a mess that obscures the boy's eyes, his motives, maybe even his dreams. As if to say that these things couldn't possibly matter to anyone else.

This culture was and is still about going out to a club to see a band and your friends. It's a social scene. *It's community*. It's about reading Peter Bagge's comic *Hate*, or yucking it up online with other fans, and it's about understanding what everyone's talking about because you've seen that new band too. Or because you've lent your couch to the same kind of loser in a Veruca Salt T-shirt who seems to move from town to town, scamming his way into shows for free and mooching beer money from everyone.

This is a community that began as a series of local music scenes, as the sort of little subcultural eddies that guys with pierced noses and goatees call "temporary autonomous zones." A T.A.Z. *is really just any place you can go to hear your own kind of music, while wearing the fashions of your chosen tribe and drinking the cocktail beverages of your generation.* It's any scene in which you can be certain that you are **not just like your parents.** Over the last decade, these little sites of youth culture began to link up, city by city, like a foundation of slightly scuffed-up Lego blocks, by sharing local heroes, ideas, and records with each other.

album art for **Positraction** (Caroline Records), October 1988

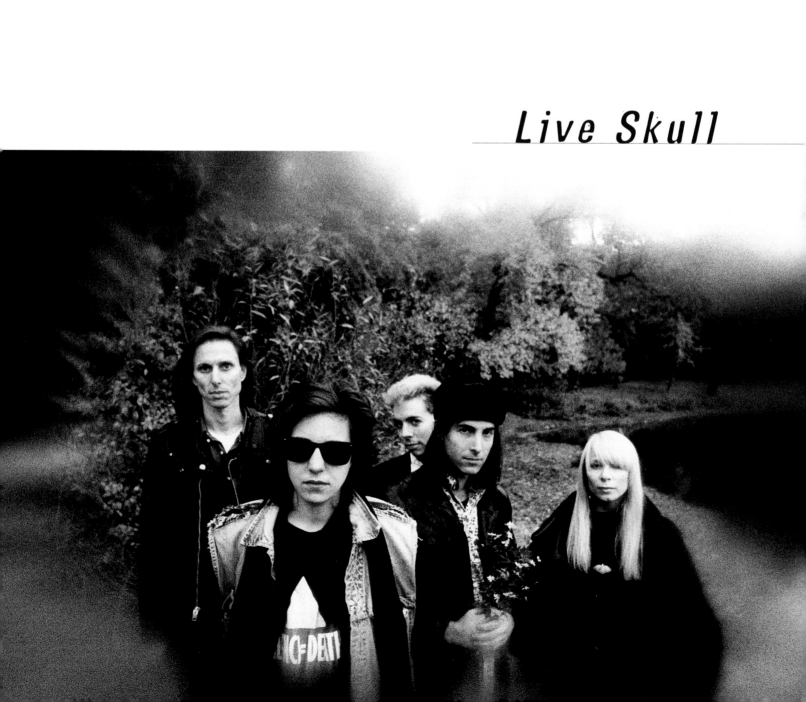

Live Skull

Deee-Lite

And there was something else that happened. Musicians and label owners, fanzine editors and college newspaper journalists, the true believers and the opportunists, all began to get curious, perhaps even *greedy.* We began to make a buck. And one of the guiding principles of punk was amended: Indie culture said, " Do It Yourself, But Buy It from Us."

Alternative culture is a self-conscious bohemia, and many of its finest artists have been very careful and very smart about how they chose to enter the mainstream. After years of making great but underheard records for small labels,

Henry
Rollins
New York City, 1991

Sonic Youth realized it might be more subversive to make their noisy, s t r a n g e music for a major label, like the David Geffen Company. And they were right. After years as the frontman of a stubbornly self-supporting INDEPENDENT band, Henry Rollins realized that if he appeared in a Gap ad, his picture, the face of punk-rock self-determination, would at last be glaring out at potential new fans from the pages of *Rolling Stone* magazine. Rollins thought of it as a kind of revenge, because he felt *Rolling Stone* had never devoted enough attention to BLACK FLAG.

And Nirvana, as they negotiated with Geffen Records in 1991, seriously considered a plan to sign a deal, then break up immediately afterward, as a way to shoot Geffen the finger and make off with a few fistfuls of cold, hard

Mudhoney

corporate cash. But instead they listened to the advice of their older, wiser label-
mates Sonic Youth and acted like investment bankers. They signed a deal that would pay off only if they sold a lot
of records. It was a gamble based on the band's intuition that their music might mean something to people other
than indie-rock bohemians. It was a gamble that Nirvana won, and they became million-
aires because of it.

Alternative is a temporary autonomous zone that never minded spreading outward, that never
stopped overflowing the grail lip of its local sponsors. By 1986, the punk ideal of cultural rebellion had
become a kind of bullshit provincialism based on who was in the underground and who was out of it. In 1996
indie-rock culture—or the alternative nation, or whatever you want to call it—isn't about being part of a cool
elite. Alternative rock is ubiquitous because it spread like the common cold: through human contact and word
of mouth. It's about infection. After all, it wasn't Nirvana that started "grunge" music. It was a band
named Mudhoney and their first single, "Touch Me I'm Sick."

Come

Option *magazine, New York City,* October 1992

For me, this story starts in 1980, when I was nineteen. That was the year that punk rock told me who I was.

I grew up in Austin, Texas, listening to the Beatles. I started *smoking pot* at about the same time that I attended my first rock concert, which was Lynyrd Skynyrd opening for the Doobie Brothers. But none of that felt like *my* music, and it was all made by these elevated beings, these untouchables called r o c k   s t a r s .   This was what I understood rock to be: a shared arena experience.

Supersuckers *album session for*
The Smoke of Hell
(Sub Pop), June 1992

By the time I was a senior in high school, I was listening to Cheap Trick and the Cars. *It was sharper, catchier, weirder, and real-er music.* It didn't sound like Yes at all. I didn't know what to call it, but for all I knew, this was punk rock, the music I'd been hearing about in all those sensational news stories from London and New York. Cheap Trick even made me want to dress differently, so I started wearing a black tie, white shirt, and a pair of horrible black slacks to school.

Austin,
Texas,
January 1993

Butthole Surfers

Soon I was going to Austin punk clubs like Raul's to see bands like the Big Boys, the Dicks, Terminal Mind, and, later, a bunch of San Antonio freaks who called themselves the Butthole Surfers. Everyone at Raul's was different from my friends out in the suburbs. **Everyone was cool and funny and scary and queer, and that was a big deal at the time.** Raul's was a scene: I knew the people in the bands, and they sometimes acted like they knew me. I began to realize that not all musicians are rock stars. At Raul's, you could watch a band, and if you liked them, you could tell them that after they finished playing, because they would be walking around the club, or hanging out, *just like real humans.*

Deb orah Harry

publicity session (Warner Bros. Records), September 1989

And I started to think about music differently as well. I found out that *the* **Big Boys** *were* **punk rock**, Blondie was new wave, and Cheap Trick was really neither. But those distinctions didn't matter much to me. All of this stuff that I heard sounded like it was made for me, about me, and, if not by me, then by FRIENDS of mine.

New York City, May 1990

We defined ourselves with the harsh, wonderfully intense and messy music we were listening to and making. It was only later that we realized that bands like the Big Boys were important to anyone else. But right there at the beginning, we knew that punk was art, culture, community, a way of life, and even a kind of cockeyed moral code. For us, **punk was everything that mattered.**

Like a lot of people who came of age in the eighties, my friends and I had grown up acutely aware that we had been born after the greatest countercultural revolution of the century, otherwise known as the Fabulous Sixties. We were told that counterculture was something made by other people, or something that was over, or something that was silly, like disco. Some of us actually believed this sort of nonsense and became Young Republicans as a way of rebelling against rebellion. But some of us, without even completely knowing what we were doing, began to cobble together a counterculture out of punk, a rebel music that had started in the Bowery bars of Manhattan, with bands like the New York Dolls and the Ramones. Those groups were the pioneers of punk rock, and for a time their innovations were borrowed, and even improved upon, by English bands like the Sex Pistols and Wire. Then punk, or rather, a nastier, faster version of punk called hardcore, was born in the United States, where it festered for a while, then blossomed brilliantly, then died out once again. Hardcore was the last, violent stage of punk, but it was also the root system of what would become alternative rock.

Bad Brains

album session for **Rise** (Sony), June 1993

Black *Flag*

performance

at Irving Plaza, New York City,
1986

Hardcore punk, as practiced by classic eighties American bands like Black Flag, Minor Threat, and the Bad Brains, was **an aesthetic of rejection.** It REJECTED ALL SORTS OF WHITE, MIDDLE-CLASS VALUES AND TRADITIONS, and that made it the perfect form of naughtiness for white, middle-class youth like myself. Punk rock was our NOISE.

But **PUNK WAS A POSITIVE FORCE AS WELL.** It was all about doing things your-self: Bands released their own records, set up their own tours, and built their own audiences out of anyone who would come to see them play. Henry Rollins described the finer points of this process in a journal entry he made in October 1981, just months after he became the lead singer of the Los Angeles band Black Flag:

album session for **Shimmer** (Atlantic Records), January 1994

"[Black Flag roadie] Mugger and I went into San Francisco early to put up flyers for the show. We were on the scam from day one. I learned a lot. I was asking him stupid questions like where we were going to sleep and when do we eat. He laughed at me and said that we were going to have to make it up as we went along . . . We met some guy who had seen Black Flag play before in San Francisco and he said that he would put us up in his parents' house, but they couldn't find out. . . . We saw Jello Biafra (singer of the Dead Kennedys) in a restaurant. We went in and sat down at his table and immediately began eating his food . . . I did my part by going to the back and talking to the waitress, telling her that we were here early to put up the flyers and we had no money and could she help us out even though we were *filthy and crazy looking*. She gave us some food and I put her on the guest list."

Rollins and the rest of Black Flag were essentially suburban dudes, indulging in an alternative lifestyle by touring the country and acting like bums. But they weren't poseurs—scrounging for meals and places to sleep was an economic necessity for a band that didn't enjoy the support of a major record company. Black Flag crashed in the living rooms of other punk bands they met on the road, and then when those bands came through Los Angeles, Black Flag found *them* places to stay. As they toured the country, Black Flag did their best to talk to fans and fanzine writers who were often just nerds with access to a Xerox machine and a passion for wild music. Black Flag's modus operandi was a pattern that many other bands, both punk and postpunk, repeated throughout the eighties. In this way, a national grassroots network of touring bands, clubs, little magazines, and rabid fans began to develop in America.

gery

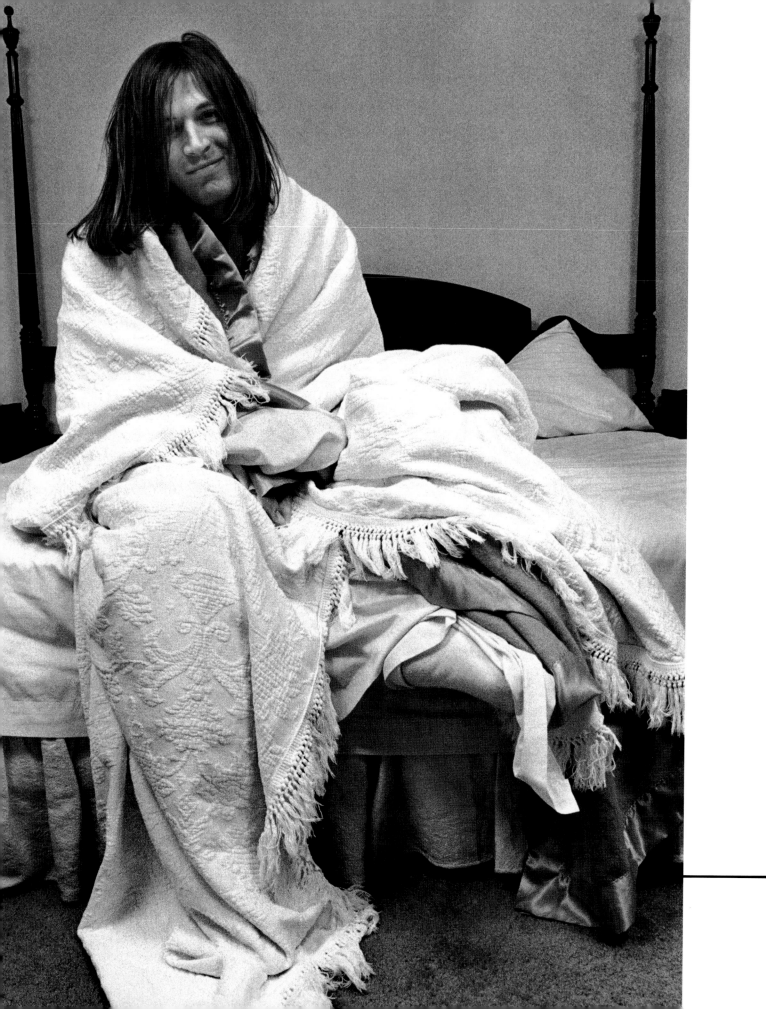

Evan
DANDO

Melody Maker *magazine*, November 1993

But a lot of people just found out about punk rock from their friends or from weirdo college roommates. In 1981 an ex–army brat and novice photographer named Michael Lavine moved to Seattle to attend Evergreen College. Once there he shared a house with two punk rockers and a Deadhead. Michael had always hated the Dead.

Los Angeles,
March 1993

X

"I was ready for something else," he says. "One of the punks gave me a copy of X's album *Wild Gift,* and then I heard Flipper, and then that made me start listening to all this stuff I'd never heard before—the Velvet Underground, David Bowie, whatever. Within a month, I had spiky hair, and I was wearing one long, dangling   earring."

MARK LANEGAN
album session for **Whiskey for the Holy Ghost** (Sub Pop), June 1993

publicity session (Epitaph Records), April 1995

Rancid

Not too far away, in Aberdeen, Washington, a **TALL**, geeky metalhead named Chris Novoselic was working at a Taco Bell. He had been taking guitar lessons, and *he thought he wanted to play the blues.* **ONE NIGHT,** as he was banging around the Bell, singing along sarcastically with the Muzak, a couple of guys came in to visit with one of Chris's coworkers. One of these guys was Buzz Osbourne, who was in a heavy, proto-grunge band called the Melvins. Buzz and Chris started talking, and that was how

Chris found out about punk rock.

"The first punk show I saw was this band Stalag 13 at a club in Seattle in 1983," Chris remembers. "I went to the club with the Melvins. It was wild, and it freaked me out. *But I didn't have my epiphany yet—that took me a few weeks.* That happened when I was at home, just lying on my bed listening to Flipper's *Generic* album. I was deep into the second side, and I just thought, 'This is *art*, man!' It just blew me away. I mean, **punk rock saved my life.**"

Kurt Cobain

Chris found out later that his guitar teacher had *another student who felt the same way about music.* This was a guy named

KURT COBAIN.

album session for **Forbidden Places** (London Records), May 1991

Meanwhile, across the country in New York City, a record store clerk named Terry Tolkin was listening to and loving a lot of these same bands, but it was all a little frustrating for him. He wanted to tell other people about the Bad Brains and the Meat Puppets and all of the other underground music he was starting to love, *but he thought the term "punk" was limiting.*

49

album session for **Nymphs** (DGC), March 1991

album session for
I Swinger (Sub Pop), November 1993

Combustible
Edison

"Actually, I coined the phrase *'alternative'* back in 1980," Terry says. "I was trying to get this trade magazine named *Rockpool* to review records by bands like Joy Division. So I told them that they should write about all these bands that were an alternative to the mainstream. Now that phrase has become the *embarrassment* of my career."

Today Terry Tolkin is an A&R executive at *Elektra Records,* and he's signed a number of **excellent alternative bands, including the *Afghan Whigs* and *Luna,*** to the label. Like a lot of the people who began the eighties advocating indie rock, he's turned his passion into a corporate job.

Spin | *magazine,* June 1990

"I am what's between thought and expression," Terry says. "It's what I do—connect people up with other people. In the early eighties, **Thurston Moore and Kim Gordon** were both coming into the record store I worked at before they knew each other. They were buying the same records, and I told them they should probably meet. Then about a year later they were inviting me to their *wedding.*"

h

Raygun *magazine* | *cover photo,* April 1993

In 1981 Moore and Gordon formed Sonic Youth, quite possibly the most influential underground band of the decade. Their music—a **_trippy_** soundscape of unwound emotion and hammered chords—redefined rock guitar playing, and their cross-country live gigging had the same impact on their listeners as that of the Velvet Underground's late-sixties albums. That is to say, almost everyone who saw Sonic Youth reacted by forming their own band, starting a fanzine, or starting a record label.

TAD

publicity session (Sub Pop), March 1988

Tolkin later became the de facto manager of one of my favorite bands, the Butthole Surfers. *Their* live shows in Austin and elsewhere were psychedelic debacles of *weird lights* and even *weirder sounds.* Sometimes it was hard to believe what you were seeing. In 1984, after one particularly astonishing Buttholes show, *I raced home,* stoked on adrenaline and dark beer, and tried to put it all down in my journal.

"King and Theresa, the drummers, rose out of the shadows like mohawked children of the Damned," I wrote. "Smiling skeletal grins in the strobe light flicker, they fell to their drums and pounded out a huge, primal beat that throbbed through the club. Paul Leary cradled his guitar and rolled his eyes up to the heavens—A sign! A sign!—*now leaning, now catatonically swaying.* When Gibby finally staggered out onstage, he was locked in a death struggle with five or nine human effigies. As he shook off the last of his attackers, he grabbed the microphone and shrieked, 'I shot the barbecued pope, I shot the princess!'"

Primus
album session for **Sailing the Seas of Cheese** (Interscope), January 1991

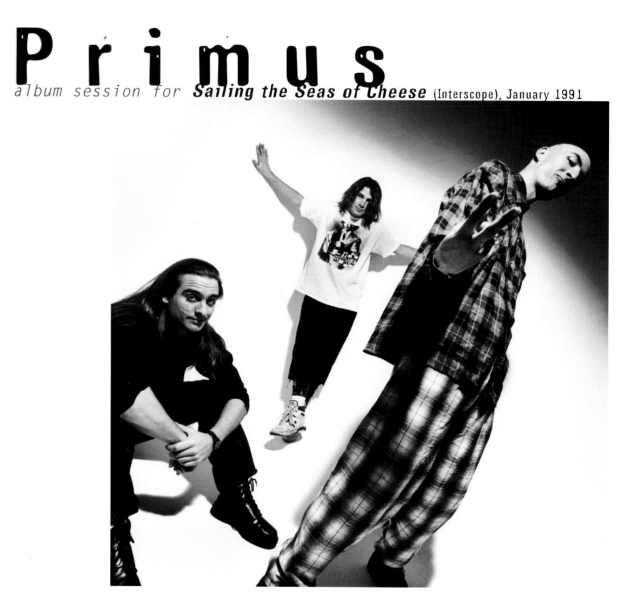

The Butthole Surfers were actually quite significant, and not just because they induced semi-coherent hyperbole in college students like myself. The Surfers were a hardcore band that was mutating beyond the limits of hardcore music. By 1984, which was perhaps Black Flag's most savage year, American punk was spawning strong regional underground music scenes and sparking other disparate musical movements. In Los Angeles, the Dream Syndicate

album session for
Smoke'em if you got'em
(Sub Pop), November 1990

Paul Westerberg

had turned down punk volume just a bit and launched a neopsychedelic music scene dubbed the Paisley Underground. In Athens an oblique, shimmering band named R.E.M. had reinvented jangly folk rock. And in Minneapolis Hüsker Dü and the Replacements, two groups who had begun as loud, fast punk bands, were evolving into something else, that is, into groups who were still loud and fast but who would occasionally sing about some pretty traditional stuff, like Budweiser beer and broken hearts.

All of these postpunk bands began by releasing their records on small independent labels. But that was sometimes all they had in common with hardcore bands like Black Flag. Punks like the Sex Pistols, the Ramones, and later, Black Flag, had so thoroughly reinvented rock and roll that they returned it to a new starting point, a new ground zero. This was exactly what punks set out to do: that's why Sex Pistols singer Johnny Rotten wore a T-shirt that said, I HATE PINK FLOYD. In fact, this anti-musical-establishment vitriol, handed down but undiluted, is a central tenet of today's alternative rock, and that's why one Olympia, Washington, independent label felt it necessary to call themselves *Kill Rock Stars.*

SPIRITUALIZED

album session for **Pure Phaze** (Dedicated Records), July 1994

Melody Maker *magazine,* November 1993

Matthew Sweet

album art for **Girlfriend** (Zoo Entertainment), August 1991

Punk meant that anything old was uncool, and it wasn't until about 1983 or so that American post-punk bands began to openly embrace rock from the past. R.E.M. was perhaps the first group to do this, because they acknowledged a musical debt to sixties groups like the Byrds, and to more obscure seventies groups like Memphis's Big Star. R.E.M. turned its fans on to classic rock music that would never become part of Classic Rock Radio, which was rapidly becoming the most ubiquitous radio format of the eighties. In this way, R.E.M, along with other post-punk bands like Hüsker Dü and the Replacements, *pointed to the future of rock by illuminating its past.*

They Might Be GIANTS

publicity session
(Elektra),
December 1991

This too was a pattern that would be repeated by postpunk and alternative bands throughout the eighties. In their music and their press interviews, musicians began referencing great bands from the past, many of whom had never been known in their own time beyond small, cultish followings. The Replacements name-checked the New York Dolls, the Red Hot Chili Peppers cited the more obscure, Hendrix-damaged albums by Funkadelic, and Sonic Youth talked about the Velvet Underground. Because of this sort of talk, any fan trying to understand Sonic Youth or R.E.M. became aware of a past underground of *"alternative"* music that was just as cool, dank, weird, and challenging as any of the postpunk it had influenced. In other words, alternative music was built from a secret history of rock and roll.

Brian Eno

Raygun
magazine,
August 1993

One of the central figures in this history, and a man who would later be name-checked by Nirvana and almost every other alternative rock musician, was IGGY POP. IGGY, WHOSE REAL NAME IS JAMES OSTERBERG, had been the singer for one of the most primitive and powerful rock bands of all time, the Stooges. Iggy and the Stooges' early-seventies performances, both on vinyl and in concert, were loud, occasionally violent displays of fierce anger and animal grace. As such, the Stooges were tremendously influential to punk and alternative music. After Iggy left the Stooges in 1974, he continued to record solo albums and tour the country playing live. And even as he began to tone down the confrontational aspects of his music, Iggy noticed a new kind of fan showing up at his concerts.

album session for **Brick by Brick**
(Virgin Records), May 1990

Iggy
Pop

"In the seventies, when pogo dancing came in," Iggy told me, "I saw it and I thought, 'God, those people went to my gigs in 1972 and saw *me* do that.' And I loved it, because I took what I did from somewhere else myself. Then, in the early to mid-eighties, the fans at my shows just kept getting more craven. A lot of that was based on my performances, which were getting really desperately wild. There's a Target bootleg videotape *where I perform in a miniskirt,* and that pretty much sums up the era. It's tremendously flawed, but I kinda like looking at it.

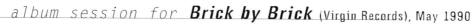

Hol

publicit
sessio
wit
Meliss
Auf Der Mau
an
Patty Scheme

September 199

Iggy Pop

"But how long can you perform in pantyhose, with *NO* front tooth, and expect people to *roll* with that?" Iggy continued, laughing. "Ya know, you can't keep telling the crowds, 'We're gonna play the "Batman" theme nine times tonight, 'cos that's just the only song I *feel!*'"

poster for **Dial M for Motherfucker**

(Caroline Records), February 1989

Pussy

back album sleeve for
Sugarshit Sharp

(Caroline Records),
August 1988

By 1987 a lot of the punk and postpunk bands that Iggy and the Stooges had influenced were either in trouble or defunct. Black Flag and Minor Threat had broken up. The Replacements had signed to Warner Bros. and lost a pivotal member, guitarist Bob Stinson. R.E.M. was floundering in bland musical accessibility. And the Dream Syndicate and Hüsker Dü had simply begun to suck.

This seemed to be the legacy of American punk rock: *dissolution, mediocrity, and failure. It looked as if our noise had deserted us.* And the tougher underground bands of the late eighties—groups such as Dinosaur Jr, Pixies, Pussy Galore—worked off this very sense of futility.

I moved to New York City in 1987, mostly because I wanted to try to make a living photographing and writing about all my indie-rock heroes. One night Michael Lavine climbed up my fire escape and introduced himself to me, because—he explained—he'd heard I had pictures of his favorite band, *the Butthole Surfers.* After that, Michael and I became friendly rivals, but it was Michael who got all the best jobs. I was doing well just to keep my pictures in focus, but Michael had this whole, you know, strategy.

"I was trying to listen to the **heaviest music** possible," he says. "**Loud,** violent, fucked-up music. That's what rock and roll is. And it just seemed obvious to me that the photography should be the same way. So I used bold colors, and I tried to shoot from the hardest angles I could find."

Michael's pictures—screaming with attitude and saturated with the color of lysergic dreams—were truly portraits of a new culture. Nobody had seen anything like them, but other photographers soon began to imitate his style. He was, at times, quite literally translating the abrasiveness of his subjects' music into a visual language all his own. Once, as he worked in the darkroom on some album cover photos of the Honeymoon Killers, Michael intentionally melted the emulsion of the color film to give the pictures a distorted, chaotic look. He didn't even know what the result of his experiment would be. *Fortunately,* the band loved the melted photos.

Michael wasn't just a punk. He was a commercial photographer, or as he puts it, *"a worker bee."* After moving to New York from Seattle, he worked for a year as an assistant to Francesco Scavullo, the fashion photographer who invented the Cosmo Girl. He learned a few things from Scavullo, and when he began to photograph shambling, frayed, and some-

album session for

Psycho-head Blowout

(Silent Explosion Records), 1987

times just plain ugly alternative bands, he infused his portraits with a hard glamour. The visual sophistication that he brought to his photographs gave his subjects a sense of themselves and their possibilities. Eventually, most of the bands that forged what we now call alternative music passed through Michael's studios, and when they got the photos back, they sometimes felt like they were seeing themselves for the first time.

Michael and I ended up taking pictures of a lot of the same bands. One of these was White Zombie, whom I first saw in a Hoboken, New Jersey, club called Maxwell's. Both the band and the crowd looked like the cast of *River's*

New York City. 1987

Sean Yseult

Rob Zombie

Edge to me—I'd never seen so much hair and torn denim. White Zombie played art metal, an ingenious cross of headbanging chords and experimental time signature stutters. They flailed their upper bodies around a lot. The singer spent much of the set lying down on the floor. The bass player, a shaggy-haired girl named Sean, never opened her eyes and never shut her mouth. I thought I might be falling in love with her. Years later, two animated characters named Beavis and Butthead would express similar feelings of affection for Sean Zombie.

"We did an interview with White Zombie," snaps Mike Rubin, who was writing for a smart-ass fanzine called *Motorbooty*. "They were doing this fucked-up take on Black Sabbath. And they had the most awesome bass player in the world. But by the time we got that issue of the magazine published, we weren't really fans of White Zombie anymore. They had become just a straight metal band, like Slayer with dreadlocks."

73

soundgarden

publicity session with
Jason Everman (Sub Pop), November 1989

Motorbooty's eventual dismissal of White Zombie was a symptom. For years punk rockers had regarded heavy metal as an embarrassing music left over from the seventies. But by 1988, metal was creeping into the sound of various underground and indie bands. Some of this had to do with the ever-widening influence of Motörhead, an English neometal band who, despite their music, _acted_ a lot like punks. And lots of hardcore icons were citing metallic seventies bands as influences. Henry Rollins wrote a piece in _Spin_ magazine praising Iggy and the Stooges' 1970 album _Fun House_ as the heaviest music ever recorded. When I returned to Austin for the Christmas holidays of 1987–88, my hipster friends in the city were listening to a Neil Young–damaged indie band called Dinosaur Jr. But my little brother and _his_ ex-punk friends in the suburbs were headbanging to Metallica.

A few groups in Seattle were beginning to fuse these seemingly disparate forms of guitar rock—the frayed and the fierce—into one sound. I stumbled onto one such band in July 1988 at CBGB's, the New York Bowery club where American punk was born. The band was Soundgarden, and their songs reminded me of dinosaurs: huge and lumbering, slow but also kind of intimidating. I was mildly interested in them and began to take pictures. After the band finished, people were practically offering me cash on the spot for copies of my photographs. A friend of mine told me the band had just signed to a major label and that they were gonna be a big deal. _I thought, Whatever._ But he was right.

Dinosaur Jr

Amherst, Massachusetts,
January 1989

At the time, I was more interested in Sonic Youth, who just seemed a lot more, well, complex. On their *Daydream Nation* album, the band was beginning to incorporate classic pop forms, like bubblegum melodies, into their psychedelic guitar frenzies. One of their more inspired moments began as a joke, when bassist and singer Kim Gordon climbed into a karaoke recording booth and taped a cover version of Robert Palmer's "Addicted to Love," surely one of the **most enjoyably stoopid pop songs of the decade.** Sonic Youth copped Madonna's surname, dubbing themselves Ciccone Youth, and then included the Robert Palmer cover as part of their experimental record, *The Whitey Album*. Their "Addicted to Love" established a watermark of irony and sarcasm that defines alternative rock to this day. And indie guitar bands ever since have understood that any sort of assembly-line pop or mainstream rock can be a sort of blueprint for reinvention. A lot of bands have subsequently made careers out of trashing rock from the past—Dinosaur Jr's music is partly a woolly revision of Eric Clapton's best solos, but by the same token, Smashing Pumpkins often sound like a feeble imitation of Steppenwolf.

Kim Gordon

Sonic Youth album
session for **Goo**
(DGC), January 1990

smashing pumpkins

Smashing Pumpkins album
session for **Gish**
(Caroline Records), February 1991

Billy Corgan

Foetus

Brooklyn,
New York,
July 1988

Lydia Lunch
Brooklyn, New York, March 1988

Some of Sonic Youth's pals and peers of the time took this strategy a little further. Jim Thirwell (a.k.a. Foetus), Lydia Lunch, and most notably, a dark, melodramatic crooner named Nick Cave were reconnecting postpunk to all sorts of dank musical forms of the past. They borrowed ideas from the Delta blues, gory Appalachian folk songs, and the opiated, torchy ballads of Billie Holiday and Lee Hazlewood. In so doing, Cave and these others authored a new American gothic, a haunting subgenre of spooky and screeching music with lyrics about serial killers, AIDS, or other modern madnesses. In the hands of these singers, a little knowledge was a powerful artistic device. "What scares me is people who *don't* have a sense of history," Kim Gordon told me at the time.

But ultimately, Kim and the rest of Sonic Youth covered "Addicted to Love" because they also genuinely liked that silly little pop song. Irreverent as it was, Ciccone Youth's "Addicted to Love" also contained an element of tribute. Sonic Youth was too smart and too aware of the dichotomy between high and low art to make truly stupid pop. But right there in 1988 they made it pretty clear that underground music shouldn't just be about experimental, obscure

Nick Cave

Seconds magazine,
New York City,
July 1992

sounds, and that mainstream music isn't just good for nothing. Most importantly, Sonic Youth was suggesting that there might be a way to make challenging and even avant-garde rock music popular. Or at least hummable.

Sonic Youth's interest in music as a populist form of communication led them to the most aurally innovative music of the times, that is, to rap. And in 1990, while working on their album *Goo*, the band was delighted to discover that they would be sharing studio space with Public Enemy.

"We really like the stance that rap music takes—not necessarily the political stance, but more like the neighborhood stance," Sonic Youth guitarist Lee Ranaldo told me. "You know, rap is coming right out of the neighborhoods, like modern-day folk music. It's really music of the city streets. And in a way, I guess we feel close to some of the sonic experimentation going on in that music. They're using turntables, we're using guitars, but still it's all in the quest of a cool-sounding thing."

Pussy Galore

album art for **Right Now**
(Caroline Records), 1987

Pussy Galore was another noisy New York band who was paying close attention to rap music. They even sampled Public Enemy's Chuck D for one of their records, 1988's *Sugarshit Sharp*. After seeing a few of the band's cacophonous live shows, I became a shameless, slobbering fan. *Sugarshit Sharp* and other Pussy records like *Dial M for Motherfucker* were full of murderous blues, misaligned garage rock, and lots of scabrous profanity. The band once recorded a song-by-song cover version of the Rolling Stones' *Exile on Main Street.* Band leader Jon Spencer seemed hellbent on chopping up the language of rock and roll, then rearranging the bits into new kinds of songs. I once made the mistake of asking him if he meant to make Pussy Galore records unlistenable.

"I don't think the records are unlistenable," he answered, somewhat indignantly. **"Why would I want to do that?** No, no, there may have been a desire on our part early on to make the music *hard*, but I think that's gone away. Also, early on, we were influenced by sixties garage punk, and my favorite records were the ones with lousy production. Pussy Galore is just music—the music we like."

Another record that Spencer was listening to at the time was "Touch Me I'm Sick," the first single from a Seattle band called Mudhoney. "Touch Me" was a two-and-a-half-minute wail of dirty, distorted guitars, hollered vocals, and shuddering, almost spastic drums. It was a song that, in 1988, sounded like the purest dose of punk rock I'd heard in years. Maybe that was why everyone in New York—including Sonic Youth, who immediately released a cover version of "Touch Me"—suddenly seemed to be talking about Mudhoney.

The band got its name from a Russ Meyer movie, and singer/guitarist Mark Arm claimed that he came up with the lyrics to "Touch Me I'm Sick" while he was watching reruns of *Hawaii Five-O*. "We're inspired by punk rock of the sixties," Arm told me. "That sorta sound and attitude: kinda basic, raw, anything with two chords. Snotty music. Songs about girls that done me wrong."

Mudhoney

By stripping their punk rock down to its most primal elements—a feral angst and a musical fury that bordered on the atonal—Mudhoney were able to express a brutal emotional honesty in their music. It didn't matter whether Mark Arm was singing about Jack Lord or about how much he missed his daddy: It sounded like he was exorcising himself. "Touch Me I'm Sick" was one of those records that felt really good because it made you want to be *baaad*. It was this very quality, and the fact that the single sounded so fuzzy and filthy, that led onlookers to dub Mudhoney and the many bands that soon began to imitate them **"grunge rock."**

"Touch Me" and Mudhoney's later EP *Superfuzz Bigmuff* were the first important records on Bruce Pavitt and Jonathan Poneman's Sub Pop label. Pavitt had spent several years working in the warehouses of the Muzak corporation, biding his time and watching trends in rock music.

DWARVES

Dwarves *poster for*

Blood Guts & Pussy
(Sub Pop), December 1989

"In 1988 the biggest band out of L.A. was Guns n' Roses," he now says. "And the band in New York that mattered the most, at least to me, was Sonic Youth. I had just quit my job at Muzak and started my own company, so I needed to know that I was gonna make a living with Sub Pop. So I thought, What can we put out that goes right down the middle between Guns n' Roses and Sonic Youth? And that record was the Mudhoney single. And then later Nirvana did the same thing. We were able to grab the great American heartland with our middlebrow rock and roll. And make millions of dollars doing it."

Pavitt and his Sub Pop partner Jonathan Poneman were devoted to the idea of recording the underground music that they loved, but they weren't exactly the Svengalis that this sort of pseudo-CEO talk would suggest. That is to say, Mudhoney would have been brilliant without Sub Pop. But from the beginning, Sub Pop was a label that clattered along with just slightly more efficiency than doomed outfits like Rough Trade and Minneapolis's Twin/Tone. They managed to send out promo records to fanzines and fledgling rock critics like myself. They began a Singles Club, which entitled paid subscribers to a new indie-rock seven-inch single every month. And perhaps most important, Sub Pop did everything with *attitude.*

Black Snakes

album art for **Crawl**

(Radium Records), 1987

"We just used irony," Pavitt says. "We made Sub Pop T-shirts that said LOSER in bold type. And our packaging, like Michael Lavine's photos of Mudhoney wagging their butts at the camera, kind of established our whole attitude. People were amused by it. They'd look at our records and think, Okay, these guys are making a joke about screwing me out of the money for this record. And then they'd buy our record."

Sub Pop poked fun at the entertainment industry even as it engaged in the business of entertaining, and this kind of irony struck a chord with more than just record buyers. Back in my hometown, a young filmmaker named Rick Linklater was busy assembling a movie about a bunch of losers who couldn't get anything done. Rick's film, peppered with more than a few Austin underground musicians, would eventually come to be regarded, rightly enough, as a portrait of a generation. But the really ironic thing about *Slacker* was the fact that the movie's director was anything but an ambitionless couch potato.

"On the night we debuted *Slacker* in Austin," Linklater told me, "we showed the movie, and then we all went to see Mudhoney afterward. And they were great. But of course, later, I got sucked up into the whole Generation X grunge hype, and people would ask me what I thought about Nirvana. I'd say, 'Yeah, gee, I *like* them, but I also listen to all sorts of stuff you've probably never heard of.' "

publicity session (Sub Pop), June 1993

Dwarves

Actually, much of what Linklater listened to then (and still listens to today) was local music, Austin punk and post-punk bands like the Dicks, Glass Eye, Texas Instruments, and Poison 13. Rick probably didn't know that Mudhoney, obsessive record collectors that they were, listened to some of the same stuff; eventually, the Seattle band began covering the Dicks' song "Hate Police." So Austin punk rock influenced Seattle punk rock, which then came to influence a new generation of Austin punks. There was nothing extraordinary about this feedback cycle between cities: That's just the way that underground culture works.

Weeze

Reno, Nevada, October 1994

Joan Jett

*publicity
session*

(Sony Music),
September 1991

Even as Linklater began production of *Slacker*, a Boston alternative band named the Pixies was recording "Debaser," a shrieking musical homage to one of their favorite experimental films, Luis Buñuel's and Salvador Dalí's 1928 *Un Chien Andalou*. The Pixies sounded like aural Dadaism: a blenderized pastiche of searing guitar work, singsongy vocals, lyrics about monkeys and blood, and an occasional cello solo or surf melody. The Pixies were a truly postmodern group, an appropriation machine that borrowed bits of ideas from everything. When I met bassist Kim Deal, we talked about movies almost as much as we talked about music.

"You go through this whole learning thing when you get to be our age, and you learn that the extremes are really good," she told me. "Like when Big Black comes on with all that guitar noise, that's really good. Or when Patsy Cline sings, and she's like *dripping* with tears, that's really good too. *Baaad* disco! You know, like the Village People: That's great because it's just so campy *gross!* You learn to appreciate all kinds of music, especially if it's extreme and the musicians really *mean* it."

The Breeders

photographed with **Tanya Donelly, Melody Maker** *magazine,* September 1991

The Pixies recorded three albums for Elektra before they fell victim to internal dissension. Kim Deal would go on to form a sly band called the Breeders. But in 1989 the Pixies were ahead of the curve, an indie group that landed in the mainstream before the mainstream was really ready for them. In Boston they were just popular enough to distract clubgoers from a quietly intense little group called Galaxie 500. So Galaxie, led by guitarist Dean Wareham, began to make regular road trips to New York City, where they settled comfortably into clubs like CBGB's and the Pyramid.

That's where I saw them. I instantly developed a crush on bassist Naomi Yang, probably because she had the coolest moptop haircut since Paul McCartney. My roommate Connie, on the other hand, started going to all the Galaxie 500 shows because she loved to watch Dean's lips move as he sang. Galaxie 500 sounded nothing at all like the shrieks of the Pixies or the grunge of Mudhoney and Soundgarden. Instead, they were

Dean
Wareham

Luna publicity session
(Elektra Records), June 1992

gently hypnotic, languid, and dreamy. Galaxie 500 songs didn't rock you so much as lull you. It was as if the band had invented an indie subgenre all its own, and some of my friends even started calling Galaxie 500 "slowcore."

"Slowcore" was just a silly label that never caught on, but Galaxie 500 represented one of about a dozen varieties of indie rock that existed at the time. In January 1990 I voted in the *Village Voice*'s Pazz and Jop music poll for the first time and happily endorsed the "shoe gazer" rock of My Bloody Valentine, the "pig fucker" music of Pussy Galore, the "grunge" of Mudhoney, and the "neopunk" revivalism of Fugazi. I even wrote a piece for *Spin* claiming that Scrawl, an all-girl "foxcore" band from Columbus, Ohio, were more authentic than Public Enemy. *Spin* didn't call me much after that.

I also really loved Nirvana's album *Bleach*. It was the best record yet from Sub Pop, and I liked it mostly because underneath all the distortion and screaming, I could hear something sort of old-fashioned: melody.

But some indie-rock mavens absolutely detested *Bleach*. Gerard Cosloy, the ever-perceptive and usually caustic head of Matador Records, wrote a scathing review of the album in his fanzine *Conflict*. He meant to say that Nirvana was a terrible band. So he accused them of playing "arena rock." And, in that much at least, Cosloy was correct. Because in less than a year, Nirvana would be the biggest band in America.

I can honestly say that I didn't see it coming. In July 1989 I saw Nirvana play live at Maxwell's in Hoboken, New Jersey. I don't remember anything about the show. Except that the band looked dirty and tired. They looked like they'd all grown up in trailer parks. Actually, Nirvana looked kinda inbred.

As it turns out, the band was simply exhausted. Chris Novoselic and Kurt Cobain were on the verge of one of the many hard decisions they would have to make for the band: They were about to fire their second guitarist. And even though this, their first national tour, had been, as Novoselic puts it, "a blast and a big adventure," he and the rest of Nirvana were a little homesick.

"All the clubs were the same—you'd walk in and smell the beer that was spilled all over the floor the night before," Chris told me. "You'd kiss the sound man's ass so you could get good sound and then play through a crappy PA. So after that show in New York, we just quit. We were burned out. We drove fifty hours from New York to Seattle. We only stopped for gas, and all we ate was powdered donuts."

Monster Magnet

poster for **Soul Crusher** (Caroline Records), August 1988

White Zombie

But even as Nirvana was beginning to learn the rules of the road, alternative culture—a cross-country tangle of bands, and adventurous college radio DJs, and independent record stores run by ex-punks, and thousands and thousands of fans—was in a state of restless germination. The seeds dropped by touring bands and by risk-taking independent labels had taken root like crabgrass.

Seconds *magazine,*
New York City,
December 1994

The music itself was mutating again: Ex-punks like Danzig and Nine Inch Nails were starting to crossbreed genres by fusing hardcore's nihilism and sonic fury to heavy metal or to industrial disco. And all sorts of indie bands, even politically righteous, anti–music business punks like Fugazi, were selling lots of records. In 1991 the Butthole Surfers released their first and last record on Rough Trade, just before that label folded. *Piouhgd* was possibly the band's worst album ever, but it sold two hundred thousand copies, more than any of their previous efforts.

Chris Cornell

Soundgarden album

session for **Louder Than Love**

(A&M Records), April 1989

Even MTV was beginning to sniff around the edges of alternative music. Impressed by the popularity of "Epic," a video by the punk-funk band Faith No More, the network began to play clips by Sonic Youth and the Pixies, both of whom had signed with major labels.

Suddenly alternative music was a newsworthy subject to media outlets other than *Your Flesh* or *Forced Exposure.* In April 1991 a slick new Condé Nast magazine named *Details* hired me to do a story on a band they thought might be the future of rock and roll. This was not Nirvana, but a safer bet named Jane's Addiction. Jane's was a Los Angeles glam-punk combo who had both underground credibility and serious rock star charisma, which largely resided in the person of singer Perry Farrell.

album cover for **Boss Hog**

(Amphetamine Reptile Records),
May 1989

I liked Jane's Addiction, but I hadn't really paid them much attention after they signed to Warner Bros. in 1988. That was my mistake. By 1991 Jane's Addiction had become America's most famous cult band. I went to see them play Madison Square Garden. The place was filled with metalheads, glam rockers, white hip-hoppers, and black vinyl punks. The place was sold out.

Onstage, Jane's Addiction was magnificent. Bassist Eric Avery hopped and skipped around like a hardcore voodoo boy trying to dance himself into a trance. Guitarist Dave Navarro alternated between slashing power chords and expansive, trippy acid rock. He was wearing a pair of silver space boots. And Perry Farrell, looking like a drug-wired lowrider, was all sweeping messianic gestures and head-bobbing manic expression. The band put on a powerful, monstrously impressive show. They looked like the new face of arena rock.

cop
Shootcop

New York City,

July 1990

Railroad

Slam dancing was breaking out in violent patches all across the Garden, and Perry Farrell just incited the kids in the audience to get wilder. "Let's fuck this place up," he said before one song. During another, a number called "Stop," Farrell just shrugged and quit singing, because the crowd was roaring his own lyrics back at him so loudly. All these kids—an audience composed of almost every variety of subcultural rebel youth—they all seemed to know the words to Jane's Addiction's songs. It was an incredibly thrilling, communal chaos.

Jerk

New York City, May 1991

I took Perry Farrell out for Indian food a couple of days later and wasn't surprised to discover that he was a fairly pretentious and utterly charming fellow. What did surprise me was Perry's insistence that Jane's Addiction had run its course. He told me he was breaking up the band, but not until after they headlined a summer tour that would also feature Nine Inch Nails, the Butthole Surfers, and Henry Rollins. He was going to call the tour Lollapalooza.

Lollapalooza became a fabulous financial and artistic success. It wasn't just a tour. **Lollapalooza was a traveling countercultural village of bands, druggy art, carnival rides, and virtual-reality kiosks.** Like alternative music itself, Lollapalooza was a collision of sensibilities—once there, you could watch a grunge band like Soundgarden, then a gangsta rapper like Ice Cube, then you could go get a falafel and talk to somebody who worked for Greenpeace. Unlike Woodstock, arguably both the climax and denouement of hippie culture, Lollapalooza was the first real gathering of the alternative nation. And it became a tribal temporary autonomous zone, where twenty-something kids could look around and revel in the strength of their numbers.

Melody Maker *magazine,*
November 1993

Sunny

Day

Real

Estate

Spinanes

Melody Maker *magazine*, November 1993

At about the same time that I met Perry Farrell, Nirvana signed with Geffen Records, largely on the recommendation of Sonic Youth's Kim Gordon. It was the climax of a major-label bidding war for the band, but just an intermediate phase in the flurry of excitement that had surrounded them since *Bleach*. Despite the forgettable nights, like the Maxwell's show, Nirvana had made a name for themselves as a radical live act who liked to smash up their guitars and equipment at the end of their gigs. Indie-rock kids also liked buying the band's T-shirts, which read, NIRVANA: FUDGE-PACKIN', CRACK SMOKIN', SATAN WORSHIPIN' MOTHERFUCKERS. And they were winning a few celebrity fans as well.

Belly

"Michael Lavine took me to see Nirvana for the first time," Iggy Pop told me. "And it was the coolest thing he ever did for me. The drummer didn't have it together, and the sound was a little off, but there was something in where that singer was putting his voice. It had an evil, devilish edge to it. It had hooks. It got into my psyche.

album session for **Star**
(4AD Records), September 1992

"The second time I saw Nirvana was at Jabberjaw in L.A.," Iggy said. "And they just absolutely wrecked the place. The crowd was just weaving in thrall to whatever song they played. The whole room was just one big snake dance."

Nirvana recorded what would become *Nevermind* in May and June of 1991. One song from the album, "Smells Like Teen Spirit," began as a studio jam. Kurt Cobain liked the song, but he was a little worried that people would hear it and then bust on him for trying to sound like one of his favorite bands, the Pixies.

New York City, January 1992

After finishing the record, Nirvana shot the now-legendary video for "Teen Spirit," which was loosely based on a couple of Kurt's favorite adolescent rebel movies, *Rock 'n' Roll High School* and *Over the Edge*. The clip was just the sort of visual chaos some of the younger programmers at MTV had been hoping to get onto the channel. In September 1991, one of them, Amy Finnerty, threw a hissy fit and demanded that her bosses give "Teen Spirit" a "world premiere" on the channel's alternative program, *120 Minutes*. After that, the clip slipped into the heavier rotation known as "Buzz Bin." And then it became the most popular thing on MTV.

Nobody, especially not Nirvana themselves, was prepared for the riot that *did* greet *Nevermind*. The band just happened to be in the right place at the right time. **They just happened to have made a classic record:** *Nevermind* was at once angry, confused, hopeful, hopeless, loud, fragile, and anthemic. And Nirvana happened to be punks. They had come up as fans of both the Beatles and Black Flag, and they had watched their heroes break up, and rage, and blossom, and get soft. But mostly Nirvana had watched the punks that came before them lose. Now Nirvana, and Kurt Cobain especially, didn't really know how to win. At first their success baffled them, because they had never expected it. And then, as *Nevermind* continued to fly out of the record stores, Nirvana began to feel that their success, whether deserved or not, was destroying the **underground** that had given them their start.

the y-men

"With us, it just happened overnight," said Novoselic. "Everything changed for me after *Nevermind* hit. And I started noticing that things had changed in Seattle. You used to be able to go down and catch shows, and you would know everybody. It was a tiny little scene, real innocent and unadulterated. It was a complete counterculture. Then you started to notice people coming in from the suburbs. Then it was totally absorbed by the mainstream culture. Everything just got co-opted."

Michael Lavine photographed Nirvana for the *Nevermind* album, for the follow-up, *In Utero*, and he even did pictures of Kurt and his new wife, Courtney Love, for the cover of *Sassy* magazine. Most of the times that Michael saw Kurt, the guy just looked tired and overwhelmed. Michael suspects it had a lot to do with heroin.

KURT COBAIN & COURTNEY LOVE

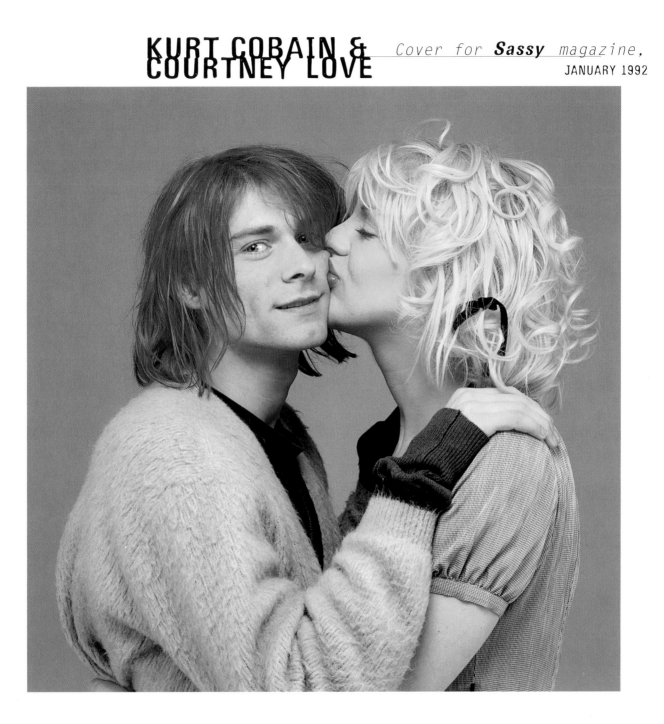

"I would tell Kurt, 'Look, you gotta eat better, and you gotta get off the drugs.' And he'd say, 'Yeah, I know,' but he wouldn't do anything about it. Courtney tried to get him to stop, and she'd come to me for help, because to Kurt, I was a guy that had been through this sort of thing. But he just stayed fucked up. Kurt was a fragile guy, but it was the drugs that killed him."

I saw Nirvana play live again in the summer of 1993 at New York's Roseland. And once again the band wasn't very good. That probably had something to do with the fact that Cobain had overdosed the day before the performance. I wanted so much to see them tear the roof off of the place. But instead I watched the sold-out crowd bob their heads and happily sing along with a disturbing new song called "Rape Me." It was creepy. Through no real fault of the band's, the Nirvana show had become a negative utopia.

Though they couldn't have intended it, there was a sacrificial aspect to what Nirvana did. As they struggled with their seemingly irreconcilable status as very famous punks, their success enabled lots of other excellent indie bands to get record deals and then to be able to make albums and tour, *just like real rock bands.*

VELVET monkeys

album session for **Rake** (Rough Trade), November 1989

Indie musicians were increasingly treated like arena rock stars by their fans. Inexplicably some of them even acquired groupies. One night in Chicago, I was sitting in a bar drinking with David Yow, the singer for a band called the Jesus Lizard. He told me that a female fan had recently offered him fifty dollars for the privilege of having sex with him. David thought the whole thing was ridiculous, but when he told his wife about it, she was impressed the girl had offered him *so much* money.

publicity session (Rykodisk), June 1992

Sugar

After a while, David took me over to the headquarters of Touch and Go, one of the most respected indie labels in the country. For the past decade or more, Touch and Go had been the sole source of wonderful noise from the Butthole Surfers, Killdozer, Big Black, and the Jesus Lizard. Now, as kids in shopping malls nationwide began to buy indie, sales were up at Touch and Go. So Corey Rusk, the label's founder and sole executive, was expanding.

Rusk, wearing a T-shirt covered with a glow-in-the-dark image of a seven-headed cobra, showed us around the place himself. He and David chatted about framing out rooms and putting up new walls, as if construction was just one of those skills you pick up as you build your own stubbornly un-corporate company.

The Jon Spencer Blues Explosion

album art for **Crypt-Style!**
(Matador Records), December 1991

cover for **"Now That's the Barchords"** single
(Sub Pop), February 1991

Urge

OVERKILL

Several days later I met up with Touch and Go's star band, Urge Overkill. And over a few martinis, the Urge boys told me they would soon be parting ways with Touch and Go to sign with Geffen, Nirvana's label. Over the past few years, the band's path had resembled an indie success story, as animated by Hanna-Barbera. They'd gone from being a fairly undistinguished, Sonic Youth–influenced noise band to being a suave trio of Cheap Trick–influenced boogie rockers in crushed velvet suits. And now they were ready to move some units.

"We've branched out since the velvet suits, into different forms of action wear," smirked Ed "King" Roeser. "We have some concerns about signing to a major label—you know, major labels are used to telling their acts what to do. Nelson, for example, don't have a vision. But if you know what you want, if you have a specific artistic vision, like the Beatles or Aerosmith, that just makes the label's job easier. We're looking for a futuristic sound. Grunge is so trendy right now, but we want our music to be a sweet experience. You listen to a Parliament record, and it just washes over you. That's what we want."

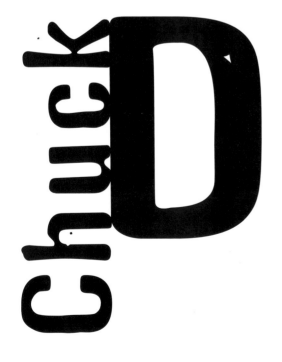

Beastie Boy s

Just over two years later, Urge would score a hit with their melodramatic rendition of Neil Diamond's "Girl, You'll Be a Woman Soon," which was the first single off the soundtrack to Quentin Tarantino's *Pulp Fiction*. But even as indie rock crossed over and infected film and books like Douglas Coupland's *Generation X,* some groups were crossing back into indie. In the mid-eighties, the members of two punk-rock bands in New York, the Young and the Useless and the Beastie Boys, joined up and began to rap. The Beasties became the most successful white hip-hoppers ever, but in 1992, in the shadow of Nirvana's *Nevermind,* the band returned to rock with a classic, hybridized record called *Check Your Head.* In much the same way that Black Flag united urban punk with suburban surfer culture in the early eighties, the Beastie Boys fused postpunk with hip-hop and skateboard culture in the early nineties.

SCREAMING
trees

album session for **Secret Oblivion** (Sony Music), March 1992

New York City,
March 1988

B e a t Happening

By 1994, the Beasties were acting like Thurston Moore, who had begun signing bands to his own new indie label, and Rick Linklater, who, after the success of *Slacker,* spent about 100 Gs on his own 35-mm movie camera and production facilities. In other words, the Beastie Boys were empire **building.** They had founded their own record label, their own boys' humor magazine, and their own line of skate-rat clothes. I met them at their headquarters, G-Son Studios, which looked like a high school locker room for stoner star athletes. When I mentioned slackers, the Beastie Boys bristled.

"Look, my generation is one of accomplishment," explained Mike D., who seemed both delighted and confounded by his role as a punk patriarch. "Our clothing label, X-Large, is a totally self-sufficient business that my partners and I built from nothing. G-Son Studios is not exactly San Simeon, but we've created our own fantasy playhouse. And the fact that it's become a reality is totally *absurd.* I mean, we've got a *skateboard ramp* in our offices!"

PAVEMENT

I've noticed the same sort of self-deprecating incredulity in most of the indie musicians I've met since "alternative" became a buzzword. Once, as I watched Michael Lavine photograph Pavement, some corny classic rock came on the studio stereo, and the photo shoot became a scene of almost unbearable sarcasm. While Lavine balanced precariously on a stepladder, trying to get anyone in the band to hold still for a picture, Pavement just danced around the backdrop, furiously playing air guitar and mugging like drunken cartoons of the Rolling Stones. It was like watching the band try to laugh away the notion that they were becoming the rock stars of a new era.

Pavement had been described as the ultimate slacker band, but singer Stephen Malkmus told me, "The 'slacker' tag is like, well, I don't know. I don't feel very slack." Malkmus had put duct tape over the stars on his Converse sneakers. What's *that* all about, I asked him. "I'm boycotting corporate

publicity session (Matador Records), January 1994

A year later, Pavement had no need for a Miller Light sponsorship, because they had landed a spot on the fifth annual Lollapalooza tour. And in the indie rock dives of Manhattan, the word spread that for their Lollapalooza appearances alone, Pavement were to be paid a cool $1.4 million.

One afternoon in April 1994, I was rummaging around in my local alternative record store when I heard the guys behind the counter making jokes about Nirvana. Actually, they were joking about Kurt, calling him "Kurt NoBrain," things like that. I thought, That's cool—they're dissing the King of Grunge.

It wasn't until I got home that I found out that **Kurt** in the head.

had shot himself

Nirvana
album session for **Nevermind**
(DGC), May 1991

Das Damen

I didn't believe it. And then I got mad, mad that this guy had taken his music away from all of us. And then of course I had to settle into a kind of blasted acceptance. A friend of mine, a writer who'd met Kurt, expressed this last part the best when he said, **"There's a part of me that can't believe he's gone. And there's another part of me that feels like he's always been dead."**

edd Kross

New York City, October 1990

Everyone was scrambling for soundbites or comparing Kurt to John Lennon. Eventually, I started to believe that those record store jokes, harsh and insensitive as they were, may have been the most appropriate reaction to Kurt's death. After all, it was just that kind of crypt-kicking irreverence that drove Nirvana and so many of Kurt's favorite bands. And as it comes, so it goes.

Courtney

Somebody once said that Nirvana meant that we'd won, and by that, they meant that punk rock had defeated, like, the System. It's a sweet thought, but the truth is more complicated. It's true that the Meat Puppets, after years of playing terrible clubs for too little money, are at last being treated like musical heroes. But so are man-ufactured insta-grunge bands like Bush, Filter, and the Stone Temple Pilots. Courtney Love is on the cover of *Vanity Fair* instead of Madonna, but I'm not so sure this is a good thing. Retro-punk bands like Green Day can now sell millions and millions of records, but the coolest and most genuinely rebellious youth that I see in the clubs are ravers, who only listen to guitar-less, electronic techno. Ask a raver about rock, and he'll tell you that Pearl Jam *is* the System.

The Jon Spencer Blues
EXPLOSION

album session for **Orange** (Matador Records), June 1994

cover for Nirvana **"Sliver"** single
(Sub Pop), August 1990

Visible **Man**

Most of the alternative bands I talk to these days are worried that television and the mass media and corporate record moguls are sucking the lifeblood out of their music. Iggy Pop, for one, does not worry about such things.

"It's silly to blame it on the record companies or the corporations," he tells me. "If you think of prison as a metaphor for society, then the record companies are the older convicts. The bands are just the younger cons. And everybody's sentenced in this thing. I hear all this talk about how 'Punk broke, and it's mainstream now.' But that sort of commentary is less exciting to me, because I've seen so many bands come and go through that maw already. I just don't give a fuck. I'm just one of those people who hears music and thinks, Is it *good*? Is it *cool*?"

Babes in Toyland

album session for **Fontanelle** (Warner Bros. Records), April 1992

The Cramps

Spin *magazine*, May 1990

publicity session (Sub Pop), September 1989

A while ago, I spent some time with a punk-rock riot-gal indie underground mosh-metal band called L7. And in between stories about their favorite concert and their most beloved memories of Kurt Cobain, I asked one of them, bass player Jennifer Finch, what the last few years had meant for her band. "It's hard to say," she hesitated, thinking about it for a second. **"It's really hard to judge the magnitude of an earthquake while you're in the middle of it. You just have to wait until it's over, and then go back and look at the damage."**

Sonic Youth

Poster for
Daydream Nation
(Blast First Records), August 1988

Raygun magazine,
MAY 1994

Lush

Selected Discography

Following is a list of records that define, explain, and embody alternative music. You won't find a lot of these listed in other record guides, but take our word for it: these records will blow your mind.

—P.B., M.L.

Blur
publicity session (SBK Records),
OCTOBER 1991

The Afghan Whigs: Gentlemen (Elektra, 1993)

Babes in Toyland: Spanking Machine (Twin/Tone, 1990)

Beastie Boys: Check Your Head (Capitol, 1992)

Beat Happening: Beat Happening (K, 1985)

Beck: Mellow Gold (DGC, 1994)

The B-52's: The B-52's (Warner Bros., 1979)

Big Black: Atomizer (Homestead, 1986)

Big Star: Third (a.k.a. Sister Lovers)
PVC Records, 1978; Rykodisc, 1992)

Black Flag: Damaged (SST, 1981)

Blondie: Parallel Lines (Chrysalis, 1978)

Blur: Parklife (EMI, 1994)

147

S

e

D i

continue

a p

BONGWATER: Double Bummer (Shimmy-Disc, 1988)

BOREDOMS: Pop Tatari (Warner Bros., 1992)

David Bowie: The Rise and Fall of Ziggy Stardust and the Spiders from Mars (RCA, 1972; Rykodisc, 1990)

The Breeders: Pod (4AD, 1990)

Butthole Surfers: Locust Abortion Technician (Touch and Go, 1987)

Buzzcocks: Love Bites (United Artists, 1978)

Can: Monster Movie (UA, 1969; Mute, 1990)

Nick Cave and the Bad Seeds: Let Love In (Mute, 1994)

Cheap Trick: Cheap Trick (Epic, 1977)

Alice Cooper: Love It to Death (Warner Bros., 1971)

Bongwater
Album cover for
The Big Sell Out
(SHIMMY-DISC), MARCH 1991

Elvis Costello: My Aim Is True (Columbia, 1977)

The Cramps: Psychedelic Jungle (IRS, 1981)

Dead Kennedys: Fresh Fruit for Rotting Vegetables (IRS, 1980)

DEVO: Q: Are We Not Men? A: We Are Devo (Warner Bros., 1978)

Dinosaur Jr: You're Living All Over Me (SST, 1987)

The Dream Syndicate: The Days of Wine and Roses (Ruby, 1982; Slash, 1993)

Brian Eno: Taking Tiger Mountain (By Strategy) (Island, 1974)

Roky Erickson: You're Gonna Miss Me: The Best of Roky Erickson (Restless, 1991)

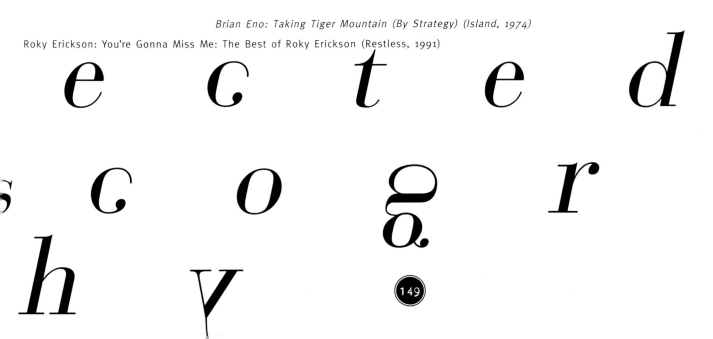

SELECTED Discography

The Faith Healers: Lido (Elektra, 1992)
Fang: Where the Wild Things Are (Boner, 1982)
FEAR: THE RECORD (SLASH, 1982)
The Feelies: Crazy Rhythms (Stiff, 1980; A&M, 1990)

THE Flaming Lips: In a Priest Driven Ambulance (Restless, 1990)
The Fleshtones: Roman Gods (IRS, 1981)
Flipper: Album—Generic Flipper (Subterranean, 1981)
THE FROGS: IT'S ONLY RIGHT AND NATURAL (HOMESTEAD, 1989)

Fugazi: 13 Songs (Dischord, 1990)
Funkadelic: Maggot Brain (Westbound, 1971)
Diamanda Galás The Singer (Mute, 1992)

GALAXIE 500: On Fire (Rough Trade, 1989)

Gang of Four: Entertainment! (Warner Bros., 1979)

Germs: (GI) (Slash, 1979)

GG Allin and the Holy Men: You Give Love a Bad Name (Homestead, 1987)

Giant Sand: Swerve (Amazing Black Sand, 1990)

Green River: Dry as a Bone (Sub Pop, 1987)

Guided by Voices: Bee Thousand (Scat/Matador, 1994)

The Gun Club: Fire of Love (Ruby, 1981; Slash, 1994)

Half Japanese: The Band That Would Be King (50 Skidillion Watts, 1989)

Halo of Flies: Singles Going Nowhere (Amphetamine Reptile, 1990)

PJ Harvey: Dry (Island, 1992)

PJ Harvey
New York City, FEBRUARY 1993

150

Flaming Lips
publicity session (WARNER BROS. RECORDS), MAY 1993

Hole

Thee Headcoats: Heavens to Murgatroyd, Even! It's Thee Headcoats! (Already) (Sub Pop, 1990)

Helium: Pirate Prude (Matador, 1994)

Helmet: Meantime (Interscope, 1992)

Hole: Live Through This (DGC, 1994)

Hüsker Dü: Zen Arcade (SST, 1984)
Jane's Addiction: Jane's Addiction (Triple X, 1987)
Jesus Lizard: Goat (Touch and Go, 1991)
Daniel Johnston: Yip/Jump Music (Homestead, 1993)
Killdozer: Burl (Touch and Go, 1986)
Killing Joke: Killing Joke (EG, 1980)

Laughing Hyenas: Come Down to the Merry Go Round (Touch and Go, 1987)

L7: Smell the Magic (Sub Pop, 1990)

Lubricated Goat: Lubricated Goat Plays the Devil's Music (Amphetamine Reptile, 1989)
The Lyres: On Fyre (Ace of Hearts, 1984)
MAN OR ASTRO-MAN?: Is It . . . (Estrus, 1993)

Minor Threat: Out of Step (Dischord, 1983)

Ministry: The Land *Of* Rape and Honey (Sire, 1988)

Ministry
Seconds magazine, CHICAGO, JULY 1992

Meat Puppets: Meat Puppets II (SST, 1983)

Minutemen: Double Nickels on the Dime (SST, 1984)

The Misfits: Walk Among Us (Ruby, 1982)

Moby: Everything Is Wrong (Elektra, 1995)

Mudhoney: Superfuzz Bigmuff (Sub Pop, 1988)

My Bloody Valentine: My Bloody Valentine Isn't Anything (Relativity, 1988)

New York Dolls: New York Dolls (Mercury, 1973)

Nine Inch Nails: Broken (Interscope/TVT, 1992)

Nirvana: Bleach (Sub Pop, 1989)

Nirvana: Nevermind (DGC, 1991)

Pavement: Slanted and Enchanted (Matador, 1992)

Pearl Jam: Ten (Epic, 1991)

Liz Phair: Exile in Guyville (Matador, 1993)

Pixies: Surfer Rosa (4AD/Rough Trade, 1988)

Portishead: Dummy (London, 1994)

Pussy Galore: Right Now! (Caroline, 1987)

Railroad Jerk: One Track Mind (Matador, 1995)

Redd Kross: Neurotica (Big Time, 1987)

NIRVANA
album session for
Nevermind
(DGC), May 1991

s e l e c t e

Lou Reed: Transformer (RCA, 1972)

R.E.M.: Murmur (IRS, 1983)

The Replacements: Let It Be (Twin/Tone, 1984)

Jonathan Richman and the Modern Lovers: Jonathan Richman and the Modern Lovers (Beserkley, 1977)

Rites of Spring: Rites of Spring (Dischord, 1985)

Royal Trux: Royal Trux (Drag City, 1992)

Scratch Acid: The Greatest Gift (Touch and Go, 1991)

Scrawl: Plus, Also, Too (No Other) (Rough Trade, 1987)

Sebadoh: III (Homestead, 1991)

Shonen Knife: Shonen Knife (Gasatanka/Giant, 1990)

Slint: Spiderland (Touch and Go, 1991)

Sly and the Family Stone: There's a Riot Goin' On (Epic, 1971)

The Soft Boys: Underwater Moonlight (Armageddon, 1980; Rykodisc, 1992)

The Sonics: Here Are the Sonics!!! (Etiquette, 1965)

Sonic Youth: Sister (SST, 1987)

Sonic Youth: Daydream Nation (Enigma/Blast First, 1988)

Soundgarden: Louder Than Love (A&M, 1989)

Spacemen 3: Playing with Fire (Bomp, 1989; Taang!, 1994)

Jon Spencer Blues Explosion: Orange (Matador, 1994)

Squirrel Bait: Skag Heaven (Homestead, 1987)

Stereolab: Peng! (Too Pure, 1992)

Royal Trux

Melody Maker magazine, JULY 1992

D

Throwing Muses

Melody Maker magazine, SEPTEMBER 1991

The Stooges: Fun House (Elektra, 1970)

Suicide: Suicide (Red Star, 1977)

Teenage Fanclub: Bandwagonesque (DGC, 1991)

Television: Marquee Moon (Elektra, 1977)

Thin White Rope: Sack Full of Silver (Frontier-RCA, 1990)

Throbbing Gristle: Twenty Jazz Funk Greats (Industrial, London, 1979)

Throwing Muses: The Real Ramona (Sire, 1991)

Unrest: Imperial F.F.R.R. (No. 6/TeenBeat, 1992)

Urge Overkill: Stull (Touch and Go, 1992)

The Velvet Underground: The Velvet Underground and Nico (MGM/Verve, 1967)

The Voluptuous Horror of Karen Black: The Voluptuous Horror of Karen Black (Beautiful, 1992)

Ween: The Pod (Shimmy-Disc, 1991)

White Zombie: Psycho-head Blowout (Silent Explosion, 1986)

The Voluptuous Horror of Karen

NEW YORK CITY, APRIL 1992

Black

Stereolab

NEW YORK CITY, OCTOBER 1992

Teenage Fanclub
PUBLICITY SESSION

(DGC), November 1991

r   *a*   (155) *p*

S E L E C T E D

D i s C O G R A

Yo La Tengo

publicity session
(MATADOR RECORDS), AUGUST 1993

P H Y

Wipers: Is This Real? (Park Ave., 1979)

Wire: Pink Flag (Harvest, 1977)
X: Wild Gift (Slash, 1981)
X-Ray Spex: Germfree Adolescents (EMI International, 1978)

Yo La Tengo: President Yo La Tengo (Coyote, 1989)
Neil Young: Rust Never Sleeps (Reprise, 1979)

contributors

Michael Lavine began his photographic career documenting the Seattle street scene in the early 1980s. In 1985 Lavine moved to New York, where he photographed such music innovators as Sonic Youth, White Zombie, and Pussy Galore. It was during this time he developed his signature style: distorted perspective, harsh colors, and extreme light effects. In addition to his work for major record companies, his photographs have appeared in such publications as *Premiere, Rolling Stone, G.Q., Details, New York,* and *Raygun.* Lavine lives and works in New York.

Pat Blashill is a contributing editor of *Details* magazine and frequently writes about the music scene and popular culture.

Henry Rollins is a musician, writer, and publisher who lives in Los Angeles and New York.

David Carson is the principal of David Carson Design with offices in New York and San Diego. He has received international recognition for his design work for such publications as *Raygun, Beach Culture,* and *Surfer.* His advertising clients include Nike, Kodak, David Byrne, *Speak* magazine, and Levi's.

PHOTO CREDITS

numbers refer to page numbers

Front cover, 102: Copyright © A & M Records, April 1989

3, 13, 48, 131, 153 (bottom right): Copyright © The David Geffen Company, May 1991

35: Copyright © Warner Bros. Records, Inc., September 1989

39: Copyright © Sony Music Entertainment, Inc., June 1993

41: Copyright © Atlantic Records, January 1994

49: Copyright © Polygram Holding, Inc., May 1991

50: Copyright © The David Geffen Company, March 1991

62: Copyright © Zoo Entertainment, August 1991

63: Copyright © Elektra Entertainment, Inc., December 1991

65, 66: Copyright © Virgin Records, May 1990

77: Copyright © The David Geffen Company, January 1990

92: Copyright © Sony Music Entertainment, Inc., September 1991

95: Copyright © Elektra Entertainment, Inc., June 1992

99: Copyright © A&M Records, January 1993

126: Copyright © Sony Music Entertainment, Inc., March 1992

139: Copyright © Warner Bros. Records, Inc., April 1992

147: Copyright © EMI, October 1991

151: Copyright © Warner Bros. Records, Inc., May 1993

155 (bottom right): Copyright © The David Geffen Company, November 1991

Black and white photographs printed by Schneider/Erdman. Color photographs printed by Anthony Accardi at Green Rhino.